CONTENTS

Introduction

1 Died on Christmas day 1891
2 Death of an infant 1892
3 Extraordinary suicide of a boy 1872
4 Death from burning 1878
5 Setting fire to a fence and hedge 1860
6 Sad story of affliction 1891
7 Revolting story from Dean Forest 1882
8 Dreadful murder and suicide 1840
9 Beaten half to death 1851
10 Scalded by boiling water 1853
11 Suicide at Coleford 1888
12 Starved and beaten by her family 1875
13 Fatal accident near Coleford 1848
14 Savage assault 1874
15 Body found in closet 1879
16 Brutal Husband 1898
17 Excessive drinking 1889
18 Throat Cut with a razor 1893
19 An unfortunate family 1892
20 Dragged under a tram 1853
21 Family dispute 1872
22 Doubtful case 1878
23 Killed by a pony 1894
24 Death by eating mackerel 1894
25 Brutal outrage in the Forest 1851
26 Buried alive 1866
27 Attempted murder at Bream 1896
28 Shooting at Bream 1846
29 Shocking death of two girls 1880
30 Death by drowning 1877
31 Indecent assault 1875
32 Fighting in the woods 1874
33 Death from a blow 1870
34 Drunk themselves to death 1855
35 Ten strokes of a birch rod 1871
36 Died from a Hayfork 1894
37 Childs Body found at the Pludds 1876
38 Attacked with an Axe 1890
39 Murder of a Toll Keeper 1851
40 Murder of a Policeman 1861
41 Centenarian Gipsy death 1902
42 Death from a cherry Stone 1883
43 Killed by tinned meat 1902
44 Highway Robbery 1912

INTRODUCTION

The Forest of Dean was a remote scattered settlement, which fostered individualism and disdain for authority. An introspective society with its own pronounced dialect and customs. Denied easy access to religious worship and education, Foresters were regarded as uncouth and ignorant and very intimating to the inhabitants of surrounding districts.

Despite certain improvements in the 19th Century, Foresters continued to display many traits of the past. They remained proud of their independence, suspicious of outsiders and fierce in the defence of their customs. Church and Chapel building and missionary work had some effect on Foresters behaviour, but superstitious belief, notably the efficacy of charms and spells remained widespread.

With the introduction of assizes courts, capital punishment, law and order the Forest of Dean became packed with curious crimes and peculiar punishments, the 19th Century was the beginning of great changes for a better life for some, but hardship and poverty for others. The Forest is still a unique place, industry that once thrived here has all but gone, along with the Railways and the old way of life. But community and a sense of belonging still holds villages and small townships together well into the 21st Century. Many old Foresters may be long gone but their remaining families still hold the strong roots of their fore fathers and the belief that the Forest is a place that belonging still matters and families stick together.

This is the second book that I have written and covers more stories from East Dean and includes West Dean. The information was obtained from old newspapers of the day, Court and Assizes records. This book does not set out to place stigma on local families but to give the reader an insight into life, its hardships, punishments and crimes that occurred in the 19th and 20th Century.

Tanya Pritchard

DIED ON CHRISTMAS DAY 1892

At the Britannia Inn Joyford, (now the Dog and Muffler) an Inquest was held touching the death of Agnes Jones aged 6. She was the daughter of William and Agnes Jones who on Christmas Day at around six o' clock in the evening, left home to go to a friend's house about a mile away. Agnes was left in the care of her brother Alfred who was around twelve years of age along with a number of other brothers and sisters. The parents had not long gone, before a spark from the grate set fire to the little girls dress, as she lay by the hearth. Alfred quickly wrapped his father's jacket around the child, but failed to put out the fire. A neighbour was called and medical attendance sent for, but little Agnes died that evening. The Coroner upon opening the inquest severely censured the parents, as some years previously they had lost another child in similar circumstances. The Jury also added that the parents were guilty of great neglect, in leaving children so young in the care of a boy of twelve. Agnes had died from shock to the system, the result of burns to her head, arms and back. She was buried on the 29th December 1892 at Christchurch.

Britannia Inn, Joyford, nr BerryHill.

DEATH OF AN INFANT 1891

Another sad story from the Parish of Joyford was an inquest that was held at Coleford Police Station, on a four month old infant John James Bourne, who was found dead in bed at his home at the Lonk Joyford on March 1st 1891. It appeared from evidence presented that the infants Father James

Bourne had come home on the 28th February and beat Susan his wife, she had left the home, returning later that evening and went straight to bed. In the morning she discovered the dead infant. Dr Trotter deposed that death was due to suffocation, which might have been caused by over-laying, or the child may have turned over in its sleep. The Jury found that in as much as James Bourne had driven his wife away, who would have attended the child, he was responsible and subsequently committed to take trial for manslaughter at the next Assizes, for suffocation of a child. John James Bourne was buried at Christchurch on the 6th March 1891, James Bourne appeared at the Court House and was later acquitted of manslaughter.

EXTRAODINARY SUCIDE OF A BOY 1872

A young lad aged fourteen, called Thomas Morgan lived at Joyford near Berryhill, with his parents Thomas and Susan Morgan, who in July 1872 committed suicide in the most determined manner. It appears that Thomas had on the day in question been working with his father in a hay-field at Berryhill, from early morning until around eight o'clock at night when he returned home. His mother Susan then requested him to walk a quarter of a mile to fetch some water, he refused and left the house. About an hour later a young lad going by the name of James Hawkins, entered the parents cottage in hast to inform them, that Thomas was hanging from a hedge no more than one hundred yards away. Thomas and Susan rushed to the place and found their son quite dead. At the Globe Inn Joyford (now under Berryhill) an inquest was held. The parents stated that Thomas had worked all day and been asked to fetch water, whereby he had left taking a small handkerchief, this was the last time they were to see him alive.

Thomas had only gone to school on and off for about eight years. He was not in the habit of attending any place of worship and had never been inside a Church, or been baptized his clothes and person were bad. He was an obstinate boy, who was afraid of his father. He frequently used very bad language and had a violent temper.

Enquires were made towards Thomas Morgan the father of the deceased who proclaimed that he was a carter in a colliery, his older son aged eighteen also worked most of the time. He lived with his wife and had five children all together in a small cottage, the rent being 1s 8d per week. The Coroner turning towards the deceased parents stated that he had never heard of a young lad of such a miserable character, but having visited the home which was filthy and disgraceful it was no wonder Thomas

Morgan acted in such a manner, and here was the Father, Mother four children and an eighteen year old son, sleeping together upon a frog grass floor covered in rags, not a superficial area to keep a pig. The children were all uneducated and perfectly heathenish, and it seemed in Christian England a case so shocking could be found. The Coroner pointed out to the relieving officer present, the desirability of reporting the case to the guardians of the Monmouth Union, and said that under the Nuisance Removal Act the place could be pulled to the ground, as such a state of things altogether could only lead to disease, misery and immorality. The Jury returned a verdict of "Felo-de-se" Thomas Morgan was buried at Midnight on unconsecrated ground at Berryhill, in the presence of a large but silent assemblage. Under Common law at the time Felo-de-se or self-murder was classed as a crime a wooden stake would be hammered into the body pinning it into place, the body was placed into a ditch, normally at a crossroads and under normal circumstances no mourners or prayers were said.

DEATH FROM BURNING 1878

Harriet Elizabeth Horrobin aged three, was the daughter of William and Amelia Horrobin. The mother had left the young girl in the charge of

Sarah Jenkins a nine year old girl from Berryhill, while she went to visit a neighbour. Coal from the fire caught the young girls clothes alight and while on the ground burning coal fell upon her, her head and arms severely burning her. An inquest was held at the Kings Head Berryhill and a verdict of accidental death was recorded. Harriet was buried at Christchurch on the 15th December 1878

SETTING FIRE TO A FENCE AND HEDGE 1860

William Taylor of Berryhill, a young boy of twelve years old, his father having run away to America seven years ago, was brought before the Coleford Sessions, charged with destroying a fence and hedge by setting fire to it, the property of Edward Machen of Newland. Sentenced to pay a fine of 40/- and 2/6d costs or be imprisoned and kept for hard labour for one calendar month.

SAD STORY OF AFFLICATION 1891

Jessie Smith Addis was a single woman of thirty, who died on the 6th April 1891. The deceased was the illegitimate daughter of Eliza Addis, who is now the wife of William Nelmes, a collier of Five Acres.

When quite young Jessie had an attack of Brain Fever, which took away her speech, and when about fourteen another attack came on, which left her deformed. She was cared for by her Grandmother at Joyford, who told the inquest that the deceased had been having several attacks of fever recently, which had left her in a sleepy condition. Jessie gradually sank and had died during the night. The Coroner was informed that sometime ago the deceased had been neglected and the Monmouth Board of Guardians had been informed. Jessie was buried at English Bicknor on the 10th April 1891.

REVOLTING STORY FROM DEAN FOREST 1882

A shocking story of avarice and depravity is reported from the hamlet, near Coleford called Five Acres. It appears that for some years an old crone called Eliza Jones, had their lived in a wretched cot in the most squalid poverty, obtaining her livelihood, such as it was, chiefly by begging. A few days ago, this wretched old woman was taken with paralysis and died. The neighbours who went to her assistance, found a canister in her bed containing £90 in hard cash, but the most revolting part of the story has yet to be related. In an inner room, was found the woman's daughter Sarah, a girl about 17 years of age, in a semi-nude condition. Both the girl and the room presenting a most horrible appearance, whilst the stench from the foetid matter in the room was most abominable, It appears that Sarah had been shut in the room for no less than three years, during which time she never left the room for any purpose whatever. The girl who is now quite an imbecile, has been removed to Monmouth Union Workhouse, where she is being properly tendered, but nothing in the way of an explanation can be got from her, or indeed anything. A very strange fact of the case, is that even the neighbours had no knowledge of the girl's existence until the old woman's death. Two sons and a daughter of the woman, living in London have seized the whole of the money found in the bed, but the Forest committee of the Monmouth Board of Guardians, before whom the case was brought, have written to them demanding the share of money due to the imbecile girl. Whatever mystery there is in this affair are buried with the old woman.

DREADFUL MURDER AND SUCIDE 1840

One of the most horrible events recorded has occurred in the Forest of Dean, which has caused the greatest and most painful interest throughout the district, where the parties were well known. It appears that a very well respected person named Phillip Willis, was residing in his own cottage, at a place called Clay End Lane, about two miles from Coleford. On Monday last, in the afternoon, he was drinking tea with his wife and daughter Anna, the latter being about 18 years old. Mr Willis was very much attached to both, especially his daughter, who was possessed of considerable personal attractions of mind and manner superior to most of those in her situation in life. It appears from evidence that Anna had got up and went outside, to bring some wood from the yard for the fire. Almost immediately Mr Willis left the room, and a few minutes later Mrs Willis was alarmed by screams of her daughter, and hastening to the door, saw her coming towards the house, covered in blood and crying out " My father is following with a hatchet," Mr Willis was close behind and with the hatchet in his hand made a violent blow at his wife, but as the doorway was very low, and from an injury, which prevented him from raising his arm above his head, Mrs Willis tried to ward him off, but the hatchet fell upon her arm and wrist. Both woman were screaming for assistance and some men working nearby, ran to the house, by now Mr Willis had put down the hatchet and headed towards the orchard. Anna was bleeding most copiously from a horrid cut at the back part of the head, which she had received while bending down to gather fire wood, she was immediately taken to an adjoining cottage and a doctor called for, but within an hour she had died. The men went into the orchard and found Mr Willis lying at the foot of a cherry tree, and in his right hand a razor. He was quite dead having nearly severed his head from his body with the razor. At the inquest it was revealed that there were two other children, who had not been at home and it was quite probable that they too would of fallen victim of their father. Dr Marsh having been called to give evidence stated that Mr Willis bore an exemplary character but in May 1840 he had attempted to cut his own throat and had been attended to, after which he was very sorry for what he had done, but agreed to be admitted to "Whitchurch Asylum" near Ross-On-Wye, Herefordshire, where he remained until his return home in July, with a certificate from Mr Samuel Millard, certifying that Mr Willis was now of sound mind. The Jury at the Inquest listened to all the evidence given and after careful consideration, declared that Mr Willis had been of sound mind and therefore was responsible for the murder of his daughter.

BEATEN HALF TO DEATH 1851

Joseph Jones was a watchmaker, living at Joyford near Coleford. On the night of the 14th July 1851 he had been in Coleford on business and on the way home, decided to call into the Feathers Inn, to collect his umbrella that he had lent Mr Harris the Landlord and to partake of a drink.

On entering the Inn, he found a group of men sitting drinking. He knew them by sight but not by name. They later turned out to be: Thomas Teague, Richard and Thomas Smith two Irishman and James Brown. Also sat with them was Mrs Brown and her daughter and Thomas Smiths wife. Mr Jones joined the group and after a few drinks, Joseph left to walk home in the company of Richard and Thomas Smith, James Brown and their partners towards Berryhill. On coming up towards the Turnpike Gate and opposite Gorse House, Thomas Smith took hold of his right arm and with the other arm forced it into Joseph's waistcoat, shaking the poor man he declared " you will give us a shilling for drink," Jones replied that if he were still in the public house he would pay for a jug of beer but would give him no money. At the top of the Turnpike Gate, Smith loosened his grip and they headed off towards Five Acres. Joseph Jones made towards his home as quickly as he could. When he was about one hundred and twenty yards away and passing between a stone quarry and coal mount, he received a severe blow to the head, which caused him to reel round and fall to the ground. As Joseph began to turn and look up he saw two men, one of them Thomas Smith, the other he believed to be James Brown. The assault upon Joseph began with the man pleading they could rob him without murdering him! He was dreadfully beaten about the head, face and body, several blows stunned him and his jaw was broken in two places, after which Thomas Smith knelt over him and picked all his pockets. It was then that Thomas Smith called out "All's Right" and they left Joseph Jones upon the ground and headed up the hill. After a while Joseph came back around and when he could raise himself a little from the ground found a gate rail lying by him, which was used to hit him about the legs, a nail from the end piercing his knee, finally he managed to get home

The following morning William Mason, Police Constable of Coleford visited Joseph and on information acquired went to Browns house, finding the man still in bed and taking him into custody, where his clothes were inspected and several fresh spots of blood on his waistcoat and shirt were found. Later that same day Thomas Smith was in a public house in Coleford drinking and was apprehended along with his brother Richard, all were taken into custody.

At the Trial of the three men witnesses were called to give evidence. PC Mason told the court that at 2 o'clock in the morning he had come across the accused and their wives in the Feathers along with Thomas Teague and had turned them out, he had no idea at that time they had committed the terrible offence earlier that night.

John Harris- Stated to the court that he had seen the prisoners running away from the area, where Jones had been beaten, he did not know anything about a robbery. When cross-examined by the court Harris confessed that he himself had been tried five times and once convicted. Several others gave evidence that they had seen the men in the early hours of the morning heading towards their homes at Five Acres. At the Gloucester Assizes Court Thomas Smith aged 23 and James Brown aged 21 were found guilty and transported for life. Richard Smith was found not guilty.

SCALDED BY BOILING WATER 1853

Milsom Townsend, a little boy aged one year and seven months was the son of John and Mary Townsend, a labour residing near English Bicknor. His parents left home as normal at six o'clock in the morning to go to work, leaving their daughter Esther aged eleven to care for him. As usual Esther did her chores and at about twelve o'clock took a pot of potatoes she had been cooking for their lunch off the fire, she placed the pot on the floor with the lid off; it had about one and half feet of boiling water in it. Milsom meanwhile was playing at the table with an onion, which fell off, he leant forward, his foot slipped, and he struck his head against the table falling backwards in a sitting position in the pot. The poor lad was badly scalded and died the following day. An inquest was held at the Royal Oak Beer house, Shortstanding and Milsom was buried at English Bicknor on the 24th September 1853.

SUICIDE AT COLEFORD 1888

Elijah Blanch, aged 51, Toll Gate Keeper and Roadman, in the employ of the Dean Forest Turnpike Trust, hanged himself in the back kitchen of his home at Poolway, Coleford. Harriet Blanch, the deceased wife stated that her husband had been suffering from nervous debility lately, and had been in a low state of health since the great thunder storm in June, which had upset him very much. She had no reason to suppose that he contemplated taking his own life, as he always talked reasonably and rationally. He was a steady sober man and had been a Deacon at the Independent Chapel for many years. On the fateful morning he had risen before his wife and when she went down she found the fire lit and the breakfast prepared, not seeing anything of him, she went into the back kitchen and there saw him hanging by a small rope attached to a nail in the rafters. She had screamed out and her neighbour Frederick Tomlins came to her assistance. They had always lived happily together and she was not at all afraid of him. Frederick Tomlins told the inquest that on hearing screams he ran to her assistance, on seeing Mr Blanch hanging, he had cut him down, but he was dead. He had known the deceased all his life and had noticed that he had been in low spirits lately. The Jury returned a verdict of suicide whilst suffering temporary insanity. Elijah was buried in unconsecrated ground at Coleford Cemetery on the 24th September 1888.

Poolway Turnpike

STARVED AND BEATEN BY HER FAMILY
1875

An Inquest was opened touching the death of Elizabeth Robbins of Poolway, Coleford, whose death arose from alleged starvation. The relieving officer of the Monmouth Union related that it was impossible to believe that in a Christian land and in a Town such as Coleford, a more deplorable case had arisen. The Jury were told that in a miserable cottage, near the town of Coleford, lived Henry Robbins alias Barmy, his wife Elizabeth, a daughter aged about 18 and two boys aged 14 and 11 who worked in the local Colliery. The only articles in the cottage were a chair, a table and a bedstead where the whole family slept, and at the time of Elizabeth's death, she lay upon the sacking, a little *straw having been placed thereon, with a covering of an old counterpane and some other trifling articles. It appears that over the last six months, the deceased had been in a bad state of health and was unable to walk on the account of wounds on her back and right thigh. Henry Robbins was frequently drunk and his conduct towards her was characterised by gross cruelty leaving his wife destitute on many occasions, as far back as September 1874, when a warrant was issued for his apprehension and he was caught and taken into custody last November. The daughter who lived at home, was no less cruel, frequently leaving her mother, and following a dissolute and bad life. When she was at home she would beat her mother on the legs until they were black and blue and throw bacon fat at her. The relieving Officer had visited Elizabeth Robbins and on one occasion in 1874, when her husband had deserted her and she being bed ridden she had promised to go to the Monmouth Union, but this had not been fulfilled. The Monmouth Board of guardians had allowed out-door relief to the extent of 4 shilling a week, but it seems that there is little doubt that she would have received it for her benefit, the husband or daughter taking it. If it was not for the neighbours she would have died some time ago. On the evening of her death her brute of a husband went to her and said: "Thee be'st going now, old woman, to* *thy right place, and hast got the ace of trumps on thy back." He then went out and returned with some clean straw with which he lay before the kitchen fire and slept while his wife was dying. In the morning he went to the colliery where his sons worked and obtained 14s as a "draw" on the plea that he wished to purchase some clothing, in order that his sons might attend their mothers funeral. With the money obtained he got beastly drunk and arrested for drunkenness and apprehended by the Police. Elizabeth's body was removed for a post mortem examination, which revealed several bed sores, one of these extending to the buttock, which exposed the bones of the hip joint, another was as large as a cheese plate. Mr Leslie Trotter, a surgeon stated that in his opinion, death arose from exhaustion, arising from bed sores and accelerated by the absence of proper living and nursing and general neglect which she was exposed to. A verdict of manslaughter was returned and Henry Robbins and his daughter were remanded into custody. Henry Robbins aged 51 appeared at Coleford and it was stated that in 1872 he had been charged with threatening to kill his wife and was sentenced to 6 months prison or to pay sureties. He now stood before Sir J Campbell and other justices charged with feloniously killing and slaying of Elizabeth Robbins and starving her. Jane Robbins the daughter was censored and discharged. On the 2nd*

April 1875 Henry Robbins was found not guilty of Manslaughter and released.

FATAL ACCIDENT NEAR COLEFORD 1848

A frightful and melancholy accident occurred to a collier on Saturday week at 5pm. Thomas Horrobin aged about 60 years of age, was employed in sinking a new coal-pit for the executors of the late Mr David Mushett, of Coleford, at a place called Howlers Slad about a mile from the Town. The pit had been sunk about 40 yards deep and 8 feet in diameter: and as the pit cart was ascending with about 5cwt of stone and earth, the rope (which was nearly a new one) broke off from the roll on the drum of the windlass, and the whole weight fell upon the unfortunate man, breaking five bones in his legs, one of which was a compound fracture, he also received a fracture to the spine. The poor man lingered till the following day when death released him from his sufferings around 8pm. At the time the rope broke, a son of the unfortunate man also named Thomas, was taking care of the horse that was hauling up the cart, he had left his duty looking after it, and it is supposed that some undue pressure from the slight neglect caused it to snap. Mr Horrobin leaves a wife and children to deplore his sudden death.

SAVAGE ASSAULT 1874

David Vaughan twenty years of age, a collier of Oldcroft, was brought up before Coleford Petty Sessions, charged with having on the 26th March 1874 at Coleford, unlawfully assaulting Mary Smith, a young woman that had borne him a child, and who was a travelling Hawker. It appeared that Vaughan had accompanied Mary Smith from Newland to Coleford, and on reaching the town, had knocked her down and savagely beat her. David Vaughan was sentenced to six months hard labour.

BODY FOUND IN CLOSET 1879

Lucy Bayliss was 23 years of age and had come from Drybrook to work in service as a charwoman for a Mr and Mrs Yarworth at Ellwood near Coleford. On the afternoon of Friday 22nd August 1879, Lucy began to act strangely, that afternoon she was seen going into the closet, remaining there for around half an hour. Mrs Yarmouth was aware that something was not right with the girl and inquired, Lucy denied anything was wrong at first, then exclaimed that she wished to go home and ultimately did.

Mrs Yarmouth spoke to her husband and they decided to investigate, and going into the closet, and covered over with soil, they found a fully developed female child, newly born quite dead.

Information was sent to the local Police station and the body of the new born child removed. The local PC for Drybrook visited Lucy's home and put her under house arrest. On the 30th October 1879 at the Gloucester Assizes, Lucy was charged with endeavouring to conceal the birth of a female child by suffocation. She was sentenced to fourteen days imprisonment.

BRUTAL HUSBAND 1898

William Pace, was living and working as a bricklayer at Barry Dock, when he was charged with neglecting to support his wife and five children, who had made themselves chargeable to the Guardians of Westbury Union. During the past five weeks Elizabeth Pace living at Ellwood had received 17s 1d relief.

William Pace stood before the court and declared that he was prepared to take his wife home again. Elizabeth turned to the judge and told him that she was afraid of her husband, who was most violent and cruel towards her. She had once had to jump from the top of the stairs to the bottom, holding her baby to get away from him, he had also fractured her ribs on another occasion.

They had been married fifteen years, but her husband at different times had left her and lived with other woman.

The court took evidence from William and Elizabeth's eldest daughter, who stated to the court that she had seen her father dragging her mother by the hair on her head, about the house and kicking her like a football, when he was found in another woman's house, he was extremely cruel to her mother.

William Pace was a man of bad character having from 1872-1897 been twice summarily convicted of wilful damage, once for playing pitch and toss, once for failing to report himself to police, twice for drunkenness, and now he was charged with neglecting his family. The Judge hearing all the evidence sent him to prison for one calendar month-hard labour.

On the 18th March 1900 William Pace was again sentenced this time for unlawfully and indecently assaulting his sixteen year old daughter Anne Pace and sentenced to six months hard labour.

EXCESSIVE DRINKING 1889

Margaret Brookes was a sixty three year old woman living at Clearwell and a drunkard. She had married her present husband William Brookes some seven years previously. It was an unhappy marriage as Margaret was an ill-tempered woman. A few months before her death she turned her husband out and then occupied the cottage alone. Margaret was prone to attacks of jaundice brought on by her drinking, her neighbour Mary Fox had seen Margaret a few days previous, whereby Margaret complained of pains in her chest and was ill in bed. Henry Fox a few days later went to see Dr Buchanan and obtained some medicine for Margaret as she was still unwell. Mary gave her the medicine and called back in the evening and found her lying dead in bed. She had no life insurance and no property of any kind. At her inquest Dr Buchanan told the Jury that in his opinion Margaret Brookes had died from jaundice, brought on by the inflammation of the liver a result of drunkenness. Margaret was buried at Clearwell on the 7th April 1889.

Clearwell Village

THROAT CUT WITH RAZOR 1893

Emma Whitby aged 42 was the wife of Thomas Whitby a shepherd, in the employ of Mr Teague a Farmer of Trowgreen, near Coleford. It appears that Emma's daughter Mary, found her in the outhouse, lying in a pool of blood, with her throat cut. She had been ill and depressed for some time. Dr Buchanan and Sergt Griffin were called, but Emma had been dead for some hours. The blood covered Razor was found and an inquest determined she had taken her own life in a temporary state of insanity. Much sympathy was felt for the husband Thomas being left with five children. Emma was buried at Clearwell on the 18th June 1893.

AN UNFORTUNATE FAMILY 1892

An inquest was held on 8th December 1892 on Mr William Miles, son of James Miles of Noxon Farm, near Coleford. The jury found that he had died from dislocation of the neck, having fallen from his horse under circumstances unknown.
The deceased had attended Coleford Fair having left home on horseback. The roads were slippery; and subsequently the deceased was found lying at the side of the road with a broken neck and fractured skull- the horse being found with saddle and bridle on in the fold yard at home. The deceased was thirty two years of age and well known Gloucestershire, Herefordshire and Monmouthshire, being a regular attendant at the principal markets held in the three counties. On all sides' great sympathy is evinced for his aged father and mother, and other members of the family, the former laying ill at Noxon when the lifeless body of his eldest surviving son was conveyed home. The aged couple have had an unusual amount of trouble with their family. Some years ago their eldest son Thomas Miles aged twenty seven committed suicide by hanging himself from a tree in the

orchard adjoining the house, and later a daughter Julia Hannah Miles aged twenty nine, was missed from home, and not without standing every effort to find her whereabouts, she was not traced for some considerable time. The young ladies body being found in the Severn at Woolaston in a decomposed state. And now comes the blow of losing yet another son, in a very painful manner.

DRAGGED UNDER A TRAM 1853

An eighteen month old little girl, the daughter of William Wintle residing at Whitecroft, met with a frightful accident while the mother was carrying out domestic duties. The little girl strayed outside and away from the home and got down onto the tram road. The child fell on the uneven road, just as some loaded trams were passing. The wheels caught her arm and dragged her a little way and then passed over her, producing frightful lacerations of the muscles in several places and fracture of bones. Medical assistance was immediately sort for but it was found impossible to save the arm. The child was put under the influence of Chloroform and an amputation was preformed above the elbow. The young girl bore the operation well and is progressing favourably.

Whitecroft

FAMILY DESPUTE 1872

Eliza Bendall alias Virgo, appeared under remand, charged with feloniously stealing a certain deed and some silver spoons, the property of William Elsmore of Parkend.

It appeared that the trouble began when an old man named Phillip Phipps had died, and was possessed of some property, the deeds of which were alleged to of been kept in a small box in his room also £29 pounds in gold. Eliza Bendall was related to the family and was called in by Elizabeth

Phipps, a young girl, the daughter of Phillip from his marriage, her mother being dead shortly after she was born. To lay out the corpse of Phillip Phipps. On attending at the cottage, it was later alleged that she had taken the box containing the deed, the object being to obtain a title portion of the property of the deceased man.

On the same day and hearing the news Phillip Phipps had died, William Elsmore, who had married Isabella Phipps eldest living child of Phillip and his first wife, turned up and claimed the property for himself, both real and personal, and asked Elizabeth Phipps, to fetch the box containing the deed. When Elizabeth told William Elsmore the box had been taken, he proceeded to the local Police station to have her charged, and believing that he alone was entitled to all of the Estate.

The Judge looking at the evidence and was told that after Phillip Phipps first wife had died, he had married his niece Margaret Clutterbuck and had a son, William Elsmore declared that this child was classed as illegitimate as the marriage was not a legal one, the Judge over ruled him and eventually dismissed the case for lack of evidence.

DOUBTFUL CASE 1878

Herbert Jenkins a Collier of Whitecroft was brought up on charges at the Assizes court, with indecently assaulting Nellie Prior Griffiths, one year and eleven months old, daughter of Thomas Prior Griffiths, Station Master at Whitecroft.

It appeared from evidence put forward that on the day in question at about one o'clock, Mr Griffiths heard his daughter crying, and told his wife to see what the matter was. Just afterwards he heard his wife say to the prisoner "Go away you beast," or words to that effect. When asked what he had been doing the prisoner replied "nothing."

Dr Currie from Parkend examined the child and as a consequence the police were told and the prisoner was apprehended at Bream. When further questioned the Mother of the child stated that, the child was sitting down in a wooden coal box, the prisoner was sitting near-by.

Herbert Jenkins stood undefended in court, and asserted his innocence. The Judge directed the Jury, that there might be doubt in the case, and Herbert Jenkins was acquitted of all charges.

KILLED BY A PONY 1894

Albert Edward Hatton, was the son of William and Kate Hatton of Yorkley. The young boy was in the

wood to meet his Grandmother Harriet Baldwin. There was a pony nearby, which on seeing the boy, ran at him, knocked him down and trod upon him, biting him through the left jaw. A short time later Albert was dead, dying from shock. An inquest was held and the owner of the pony Mary Ann Grace, stated to the hearing that the pony was about eight years old, she had purchased it from a traveller a fortnight previous, but took no warranty. She went on to say that the man who she had brought it from, said it would foal in about a week and that at such times the pony was vicious. Mrs Grace went on to explain that the day before the incident, her own child had fed the pony, though she agreed that it was wicked.
The Jury found Mary Ann Grace guilty of negligence, in allowing the pony into the Forest, knowing it was wicked. Albert was buried at Viney Hill on the 20th May 1894 aged 2

DEATH BY EATING MACKREL 1894

An inquest was held at Parkend touching the death of Ernest Macey three years and upwards in age. Ernest was the son of Thomas Macey, general labourer living at no 3 The Square, Parkend. It appeared from evidence from the Father and Annie Knight, housekeeper, that on the Monday evening *she had served mackerel for dinner, of which three children and herself partook. Subsequently Ernest was seized with vomiting and diarrhoea and died before Dr Haplin could reach him.*

Dr Haplin deposed that in his opinion the vomiting and diarrhoea were caused by eating the mackerel. He concluded that he considered mackerel to be an unsatisfactory food unless fresh and a verdict was accepted with the medical testimony. Ernest was buried at Parkend on the 27th May 1894 alongside his mother who had died from Placenta Praevia Haemorrhage a few weeks later after giving birth to Ernest.

The Square, Parkend

BRUTAL OUTRAGE IN THE FOREST 1851

In 1851 Mary McCarthy a miserable, way-worn woman of about 35 years of age, was "tramping" from Coleford to Gloucester. She was suffering from cold, hunger and fatigue. At about ten o'clock at night she saw some charcoal fires giving light in the nearby Forest, she proceeded to one of them sat down in front of one, with a view of resting herself and drying her wet clothes. She remained there until around one in the morning, when two charcoal burners arrived, who were followed shortly after by several others. They at first appeared to treat her kindly and one offered to take her to a near-by public house, Mary declined, but asked for a cup of water instead. He did so and then once she had drunk it she was offered a place to sleep in a nearby cabin. The cabin belonged to Richard Kear who promised her that she would be safe. Mary refused at first, but the men forced her to go and once inside they secured the door.
The nine men, one after the other, brutally assaulted and violated her, leaving her more dead than alive from the effects of the brutal treatment she had experienced. They turned her out and she cried for help, to which she was told that if she did not hold her tongue she would be thrown on the fire, she fainted and when she came round, was told

to leave or she should have her head smashed in with a shovel.

The poor woman struggled onto her feet and headed in the direction of Blakeney, It was daylight and Ann Jenkins was travelling along the road, she observed a woman in pain and crying, she inquired as to what was wrong and was shocked when Mary told her what had happened. Exhausted Mary could walk no more and laid down under a hay-rick where she remained until the afternoon, when PC Ellison arrived and conveyed her to Westbury On Severn Workhouse, after finding her in an almost dying state and scarcely able to move.

Mr Bumble, the Medical Officer attended to her that same evening and found her to be in a dreadful state and very ill, as a woman would be from such treatment she had received. She declared to him that she was passing through the Forest searching for her brother, she had one child, though not married but she had never lived by prostitution.

The Police began their search for the nine men, within hours they had apprehended Richard Kear 24 of Yorkley, James James aged 28, Thomas James aged 21, George Charles aged 22 and Thomas Stephens aged 20. All five men were committed for trial and received sentences from 15years to life and transported to Bermuda Penal Colony. Four other men appeared to of disappeared and a year after the above trial, Hiram

Archer from Pillowell aged 26 who was caught living in Bleanavoun under an assumed name of Evans and Henry Shapcott aged 18 were apprehended. There was no sign of the other two men. Hiram and Henry appeared in Court charged with the rape upon a poor Irishwoman, both were transported.

It is believed that some of the above men returned to the Forest some years later.

Charcoal Burning

BURIED ALIVE 1866

A distressing accident happened to a man named William Vaughan near Viney Hill. Deceased was getting stone from a bank at the lane side leading from the Purlieu to Oldcroft, he had undermined the earth and obtained probably a wagon load of stones, an oak tree stood above that part which he had cut away, and he was cautioned to be careful lest the tree should fall, and on the Friday it fell, bringing with it a considerable portion of the overhanging earth. On the Saturday Vaughan went to work as usual taking his dog. At about one o'clock the deceased wife went up to the quarry with his dinner; she could not find her husband, but noticed his coat and the dog nearby, she endeavoured to get the dog, but he would not move, she noticed that a quantity of rubbish had fallen upon the working in the quarry, and presumed her husband had gone for help, and returned home.

In the course of the afternoon, a relation hearing about the above, was apprehensive that something serious had happened and she went to the place. The faithful dog was still sitting on the bank occasionally howling, having looked at the earth that had fallen, she felt certain her brother-in-law was under it. Ultimately assistance was obtained, and after removing a few barrows full of earth William Vaughan's body was found. The sad news soon spread and Williams's wife on hearing it became insensible. A great number of persons hastened to the spot, among them a grown up daughter of the deceased, her shrieks upon seeing her father were heartrending. The dog who had not forsaken his master now wailed in a piteous manner. It was found that William was quite dead; his head was frightfully smashed. The deceased was conveyed home. William was buried on the 19th September 1866 aged 47

ATTEMPTED MURDER AT BREAM 1896

The Village of Bream was aroused by a rumour of attempted murder! The parties concerned were two brothers William and George Crote. There had been an on-going grievance between the two, and on the night of 16th September 1896 at around eleven o'clock at night, George left the Inn where he had freely been drinking and made his way to his brothers cottage armed with a broken scythe. Outside he shouted and challenged his brother William, intimating his intentions "to do him in." William at once went out and disarmed him and followed him up the path, it was dark and William tripped over a shovel and fell upon his brother, who drew out a pocket knife, slitting him across the throat, inflicting a wound about four inches long, not content he began to hack at William causing eight to nine wounds. By now Williams wife and neighbours were upon the scene and the knife was taken from him. William was taken at once to the nearby doctor to have his wounds attended. PC's Waite and Hagget of Parkend, were communicated with and George Crote was remanded in custody at Coleford Police Station. William survived the attack although unable to work for many months, eventually made a full recovery. On the 24th September George appeared before the magistrates charged with inflicting grievous bodily harm to

William Crote and was imprisoned for four calendar months.

SHOOTING AT BREAM 1846

An inquest was held at Bream on the body of Thomas Isaacs aged about 11, whose death was occasioned in the following manner.
Three men called Thomas Brown, William Beach and George Ridler having two guns with them, had been amusing themselves shooting at small birds. After a while they adjoined to the Cross Keys Inn, Bream and drank two quarts of beer between them, before leaving to proceed home. As they passed along the road, a bird alighted within distance for a shot. Ridler said " shot the whoop" meaning the bird, upon which both Brown and Ridler raised their guns and fired.
Only Ridlers gun, however went off, that of Browns having hung fire, but this he did not seem to be aware of. Indeed all three men believed at the time that both guns had exploded. While looking for the bird the boy Isaacs came up, and as he approached them, Brown said "I'll have a bit of fun with the boy" and called out to him. "I'll shoot you my boy." Isaacs stood still and laughed, Ridler asked him "where are you going to my little man." To which Isaacs replied, "down to Richard Morgans to have my dinner." All the time Brown, who was

about a yard from the boy, continued his most unhappy frolic, still pointing the muzzle of the gun backwards and forwards in front of the child, when at last the gun went off, and lodged the contents in the breast of the ill-fated boy, who at once put his hand to his chest and cried out!

Brown was horror stricken at what he had done and running to the little fellow, took him in his arms and said "My dear child, I would not of done this for the world, I thought the gun was empty." They carried the boy to a nearby cottage and Ridler proceeded with haste to Coleford for a Surgeon, but long before his return the deceased breathed his last sigh. Thomas was buried at Bream on the 17th December 1846.

SHOCKING DEATH OF TWO GIRLS 1880

At the Kings Head Inn, Bream an inquest was held on the bodies of Sarah Jane Shingles aged sixteen and her sister Kate aged seven, the daughters of James and Sarah Ann Shingles, who were killed the previous evening.

William Jones, a waggoner in the employ of Mr James Hughes of Bream Lodge, deposed that on the previous day he was in charge of a timber wagon drawn by three horses. He was returning home from Lydney and was near the Leech Pool, *when he saw some girls with burdens of wood. They asked him as he was passing if they could put the burdens on the wagon in which he replied "It was not safe for them to ride because of the pole" They told him "We shall not get hurt" and three of the girls rode on the pole inside of the wheels, the fourth at the tail of the wagon.*

He drove to Bream Grove weighing machine and then on towards Bream, on getting near the bottom of the hill he ran over some nearly broken stone which gave a little jerk on the waggon and the horses ran on, he looked back to make sure the bundles were safe and could see the three girls had come off the wagon the fourth girl was still sat on the tail. He stopped the wagon, and then saw the girls on the ground. Two of the girls, Sarah Jane and Kate Shingles were taken to the nearby cottage of Mrs Watkins, neither spoke and both died almost immediately, the third girl had her legs run over. John Preest who was walking on the road observed the accident and at the inquest told the jury how the three girls had fallen backwards off of the pole and the hinder wheel went over the two deceased girls. He believed the wheel went over the elder girls head and as stated both died almost immediately. The verdict at the inquest found the girls had been accidently killed by falling off and being run over by a timber wagon. Sarah Jane and Kate were buried at Bream on the 16th May 1880

St James Bream

DEATH BY DROWNING 1877

At the National School Bream, an inquest was held on the body of Edith Wall, infant daughter of Mr Edward Wall, School Master of this place, who was drowned in a small tub of water.

According to evidence given Edwards older daughter Annie was at home and looking after the child and doing some house hold chores, about midday Annie noticed that Edith was not in the house and calling out for her, noticed the back door open, having gone outside, she found the child laying over a small tub, with her face immersed in water. The parents were called from the School close at hand, who on arrival found their young daughter Edith dead. The child was buried on the 6th June 1877 aged 18months at Bream

INDECENT ASSAULT 1875

Christopher Israel James, a young collier of Mosley Green, was charged with attempting to unlawfully, violently and feloniously assault a young girl called Mary Jenkins aged twelve.
It appeared that Charles had lodged at the home of the girl's mother, a widow for more than two years. On the night of the 26th January 1875, Mary's mother had left the cottage leaving her daughter and Charles eating his supper. At a short time later, according to evidence he made an indecent assault upon the girl, he was apprehended and committed for trial. On the 18th February he appeared at the Gloucester Assizes and was acquitted of the charge.

FIGHTING IN THE WOOD 1874

William Morgan, William Stephens, James Ambury and William Vaughan alias "Ruffian," were all drinking at their local Public House the Rising Sun at Mosley Green. They left just before eleven one night to cross the common on the way back to their homes at "The Barracks" and argument between Morgan and Stephens erupted and soon the pair were challenging each other to a fight. All four men proceeded to the near-by enclosure and a fight between Morgan and Stephens ensured. Morgan drew a knife on Stephens and pierced him through the bowels, who on losing blood from the wound, fainted and was carried home. Dr Currie attended and the following day William Morgan aged about 24 was apprehended and formerly charged at Coleford Police Court, where he was remanded for the attendance of the prosecutor, who was too ill to be present. Morgan had already been in trouble the year previous where he was found guilty of unlawfully threatened and intimidated one James Brown on the 5th of May 1873 and was sentenced to seven days hard labour.

"The Barracks" Mosley Green

DEATH FROM A BLOW 1870

An inquest was held at Woolaston, on the body of Mary Murphy, whose death appeared to of been caused by a blow to the head, given with a small stick, by a young man named Frederick Cook, who resides at the same place.

First called to give evidence was Sarah Ann Williams, a girl aged eleven, who told the Jury that she knew it was wicked to tell an untruth and said " I live near the Carpenters Arms, Last Friday I saw Mary Murphy and I know Frederick Cook, I saw both of them up the Primitive Chapel, that's where he beat her, she was coming up with water from the well. I saw him beat her with a stick, the stick was as big as my little finger. He hit her twice on the head both sides, on the back and shoulders. She cried out and headed in the direction of her home. I also saw Leech he was throwing dirt in the water."

John Murphy Father of the deceased was then called upon to give evidence.

"I am a Farm Labourer, working and living in Woolaston. The deceased was my child, and eleven years of age. I was not at home last Friday when she came home; I did not return to my cottage until around seven at night. At supper time, she came and sat alongside me and said." "Oh dear! I have got the headache."

Mr Murphy carried on, "After Supper she complained of having been beaten, I had felt the top of the head, there was a small lump; I told her to go to bed, and she went about half past nine, between one and two o'clock in the morning, I heard her screaming, I went to her room but found her asleep, at about half past four, I spoke to her; she then complained of the headache, I left and went to work, but never saw her alive again."

Woolaston Chapel

Frederick Cook was next called and cautioned by the Coroner. He said "I am a tiller and plasterer and live at Woolaston Common. I knew the deceased, and saw her on Friday last, she was near our home at the well, throwing stones into the water." "I said, you had better give over throwing stones into the well; it does not belong to you at all." "I had no stick in my hand, I have no more stick than I have now."

The Coroner asked if he had heard the last witness's statement and Frederick replied no. The Coroner then told the accused that she had told the Jury that she had heard him say to the deceased, "That you would knock her head off, and that you struck her twice on the head, shoulders and back."

Accused: "I said nothing of the kind!
Coroner: "Will you positively swear that?
Accused: "Yes, I never struck her in my life"
Sarah Williams was recalled.
Coroner: "Frederick Cook did you see this girl?"
Accused: "I did not"
Coroner: "Sarah Williams, Is that the man you saw strike the deceased with a stick."
Sarah: "Yes Sir"
Accused: "She was not there."
Coroner: "Are you quite sure you saw Cook there?"
Sarah: "Yes Sir."
Coroner: "Are you quite sure you was there?"
Sarah: "Yes Sir."

The Coroner turned back to Cook asking him again, if he had struck the child, had he heard her cry out and again he his reply to the Jury was that *he did not strike the child or hear her cry out, and furthermore he was not there more than a few minutes as he was going to help his Father out in the house.*

Sarah Williams was examined again, and asked how far from the Chapel is the well, had she seen the deceased throwing stones into it, and where had Cook struck her.

Cook admitted seeing Mary Murphy by the Chapel with a boy named Leech, who was his nephew, as he was on the way to help his Father.

The Coroner then began another round of questioning:

Coroner: "Seeing the deceased and Leech what did you say?"

Cook: "I saw deceased and my nephew crying, he told me that Mary Murphy had been beating him, I told the deceased I would get a stick about her, I did not do so, I had no stick in my hand."

The Surgeon who made the post mortem examination took the stand, and told the hearing that he had examined the body the previous day and had found small bruises on the left shoulder and an older one. There was an external mark on the head and two extravasations of blood, one on top of the forehead, the other on the crown, which could have been caused by a stick. The cause of death being Congestion of the brain.

Jane Davies Aunt to the deceased told hearing that she had seen her niece on the Friday and appeared in good health, on the following day she saw her lying in the gutter, she appeared to be very ill and died about three in the afternoon.

Mr Motteram who was present for Frederick Cook, addressed the Jury and stated that in his opinion, Sarah Williams spoke merely from what she had heard, and not from what she had seen. There was no evidence Cook had struck the deceased.

He also reminded the Jury that Mary Murphy had more care and labour placed upon her, than was fitting for so young a child, looking after her younger sibling and carrying about a two year old in hot weather, without neither hat, nor bonnet. He further went on to say there were cases of sunstroke that brought on congestion of the brain that can happen without a blow to the head being given.

The Judge after listening to the evidence summed up the case as follows:

Death may have been caused by a slight tap, which by the heat of the sun caused death, but he believed that Cook was guilty of the offence.

The Jury after a short consultation returned a verdict of Not Guilty. An applause was attempted, but immediately quelled.

Mary Murphy was buried 16th June 1870

DRUNK THEMSELVES TO DEATH 1855

Two men, Charles Walker a Stonemason aged nineteen and Samuel Hawker a labourer aged 29, both from Lydney, drank themselves to death over a wager of drinking Raw Rum, for half a sovereign in the presence of several persons, who, shockingly to say, instead of preventing the disgusting act, actually encouraged its fulfilment.

At about Midday the two men, already under the influence of liquor, went into the Cross Keys Beer house, which was filled with people that had come to Lydney Fair and turning towards Walker, Samuel Hawkins challenged him to drink, three half pints of raw rum, in five minutes and whoever put the other out of the door would be the winner of half a sovereign. Walker accepted the challenge and his uncle William Munday, put down a coin on the table to seal the bet, while William Edwards went to fetch three pints of raw rum from the Feathers Inn.

The men drank the rum within minutes and Hawkins fell senseless to the floor, Walker dragged him outside the beer house, so that he could claim the money. Hawkins was taken home. Walker re-entered the beer house and also became insensible from the effects. Both men were dead by the following morning from drinking themselves to death and buried the same day on the 11th November 1855 at Lydney.

Cross Keys Beerhouse

TEN STROKES OF A BIRCH ROD 1871

Frederick William Ellis aged ten years the son of Jane Ellis of Lydney, was charged with feloniously stealing a purse containing five pounds and twenty four postage stamps. Sentenced to fourteen days hard labour and whipped with ten strokes of a birch rod.

DIED FROM A HAYFORK 1894

At the reading room Aylburton on the body of Frederick Jones aged 35, who died on the 2nd July after being pricked in the chest by a point of a *hayfork. Dr Carter explained to the inquest that the prong of the pike had pierced the right lung, and death had resulted from a Haemorrhage. It was also mentioned the deceased was one of a family of five brothers, and he was the fourth who had met a violent end.*

Alyburton

CHILDS BODY FOUND AT PLUDDS 1876

In September 1876 Elizabeth Hale was doing work in her brother's garden at the Pludds near Ruardean, when she was alerted to a dog gnawing at something. Elizabeth fetched her sister-in law Emma and together on approaching the dog, believed it to be gnawing on a child's head.

Alarmed they called for Moses Hale who beat off the dog and PC French was called to come at once. On further examination of the spot, PC French took possession of the remains which was delivered for a post mortem.

An inquest was opened by M.F.Carter at the School Room Lydbrook, where from evidence given by Dr Fletcher who examined the remains of, a head, portion of neck, heart, liver, spleen and a portion of intestine that the body could not be identified as either male or female, but would have been about nine days old. He could not say whether the child was born alive or dead.

On further investigation a single woman called Sarah Ann Baldwin was apprehended and charged with concealment of a birth. On the 22nd March 1877 Sarah appeared at the Assizes Court and found guilty, she was sentenced to 14 days hard labour. Sarah Ann went on and married John Brown Read

ATTACKED WITH AN AXE 1890

Littledean is one of the oldest villages in the Forest of Dean, and it is upon Whit-Monday that the annual fair is held.

In one of the public houses in Littledean called the Kings Head, George Wynn a retired chimney sweep sat, he was a bit of a curiosity in his ways and a warm supporter of the Conservative cause and was proud of his "Blue blood."

George lived in the main street of Littledean, with his granddaughter who helped as his housekeeper. Another couple who were sat in the public inn were Samuel and Elizabeth Damp a middle aged couple who had moved to Littledean some two years previous and lived a few doors down from George Wynn.

Towards the evening, George arose and left to go home. Around eight his daughter in law called at the house, but finding the front door locked she made her way to the back door which was open and discovered the poor man, flat on his back on the kitchen floor, motionless but still alive. The alarm was raised and PC Eagles who lived just around the corner was summoned to attend. A number of neighbours had by now assembled and among those enquiring were Mr and Mrs Damp.

Mr Wynn was lifted up, and on seeing Samuel Damp at once accused him, as much as his speech would allow of the attack upon him. A lathe axe was handed to the Officer and Wynn declared it was the weapon used upon him. The formidable instrument told its own tale, it was covered in blood, and on the cutting edge were several human hairs, the same colour as Wynn's.

Damp appeared much excited but denied all knowledge of the crime, and asked what reason there was that he should be suspected.

PC Eagles, however, in the face of such evidence could do no less than detain both Damp and his wife, and they were shortly lodged in the lockup at Littledean. While all this was going on PC White had gone to Cinderford and at around ten O' Clock returned with Dr McCartney, who found Wynn in a very dangerous state, his head had been chopped all over, and it presented a shocking and sickening spectacle. Some of the cuts very in a very dangerous locality, and the wonder was that the man was still alive. The wounds were sewn up and bandaged and George was put to bed. Dr McCartney stated that in his opinion George was in grave danger of dying and as a consequence, Mr Bright a Cinderford Magistrate was brought down to the house around midnight, where in the bedroom George lay, the prisoner was brought in and identified as the man who had murderously attacked him. Samuel Damp was then returned to the lock up.

During the night it was discovered that money was missing from the house and on searching the prisoners no money was found upon their persons. A few days later at distant intervals George Wynn began to recall the events. On the Whit-Monday during the day he had quarrelled with Samuel Damp and his wife, he also remembered that on his return home, he was dozing in his chair and twice Samuel Damp had come into the Cottage which had aroused him. On the third time he awoke to find himself hacked over the head with his own axe. PC Eagles on entering Samuel Damps home, came across an amount of money, later identified as the money taken from Mr Wynn's home.

The Prisoners were interviewed and it soon became apparent that Samuel and Elizabeth Damp were not married and her real name was Elizabeth Bowden a Hawker and native of Liverpool and the illicit lover of Samuel Damp. It was also clear that Samuel was not a Marine Store Dealer, but a rag and bone collector originally from Hare Lane Gloucester who had already served time in prison for various deeds. Both Samuel Damp and Elizabeth Bowden were charged with attempted murder of George Wynn and while awaiting trial at the Assizes Court in Gloucester, Samuel Damp escaped from Littledean Prison. Damp had been put in the airing yard for exercise by PC Eagles, who immediately went back into the prison building to discharge other duties, Damp saw his chance and vaulted some iron rails, which were about eight foot high, there gaining entrance into the outer yard, here he came across a ladder which was being used for some building work and he was able to make his escape by climbing the ladder and scaling the boundary wall.

A search party was soon underway when it was discovered that Damp had absconded, but no sight of him was made, until he was spotted and apprehended in a nearby wood nearly a week later cold and hungry.

When the case came up in Court, Elizabeth Bowden was discharged but Samuel Damp was found guilty of attempted murder and theft and sentenced to fifteen years penal servitude at Her Majesty's convict prison Portsmouth. George Wynn survived and died four years later aged 73.

Broad Street, Littledean

MURDER OF A TOLL KEEPER 1851

The Turn Pike at Littledean End Lane was kept by a man named Robert Hartland. About a month before October 1851, Hartland had caused the apprehension of a man named Young, who lived about 300 yards from the Turn Pike on a charge of fowl stealing. Young was committed to trial, but the Magistrate admitted him to bail until the sessions. It was supposed that a good deal of ill feeling arose towards Hartland on the part of Young and his companions, although it did not appear that any open threats were made use of by them.

On the 11th October 1851, being a Sunday Hartland became alarmed at hearing stones being thrown violently against the door of the Toll House, and he immediately went out into the road to see what the matter was. He could see nothing; but just as he was turning into his cottage, he was startled by the sound of gun fire and immediately after knew he was shot. He managed to raise the alarm and was carried into the Toll House and the Police sent for.

An examination was made of the area and footprints were discovered on the other side of a hedge across the road, about 15 yards from where Hartland was shot, The Police Officer also found a leaden bullet close by the side of the Toll House. The Officers followed the footprints which led them to a cottage inhabited by William Young Snr, William Young Jnr, Amos Young, and James Williams-son in law and Joseph Probyn. They were all rounded up and taken into custody and a search was made of the cottage where secreted away was found a smock frock and a hat, which appeared to of been used as a disguise, also found was a leaden bullet, exactly similar in make and size, which had been found at the Toll House.

The Police kept stick watch on the cottage all night and in the morning they observed a man named James Gwilliam loitering on the outskirts of the garden, and on apprehending him, they found on his person a gun barrel, which had evidently been in a fire, as if the stock had been burnt away, and which was still warm. Gwilliam was lodged in the prison with the others.

A few days later Hartland died and a further search of Young's cottage was made and the lock and pins of a gun were found secreted in an oven.

An inquest was opened and the Jury told that Robert Hartland had died from a bullet that had entered his stomach, but had got lodged in his hip, injuring the Great Arteries. Witnesses were called to the Inquest as follows:

Thomas Cox a labourer of Littledean stated that on Saturday 11th he and his wife had left their home at around five fifteen in the evening to go to see his Father in Law who lived on Popes Hill. At the Toll House he had seen Robert Hartland and spoke with him. We then went across by prisoner Young's garden; I saw old William Young in the garden by the potato heap; he was dressed in a long dirty smock frock, very much like the one produced, and a low crowned hat, like the one produced. There was two/three others talking to him.

On our return from popes hill which we left about seven fifteen, we came to the gate leading into the Chestnut enclosure, I put down my basket to rest myself and that's when I saw Amos Young in between a walk and a run in the direction of Popes Hill. I said "How do you do Mr Young" he answered and went on. He was dressed in a dark jacket and I saw a young woman Ann Gardner meet him. When we were opposite Young's house, Old Young came out of the bushes where there was no road; he was walking from the Toll Gate; when he saw us he came upon the path, he was walking fast and seemed quite excited. William Young was then dressed very differently from when we had seen him earlier, he was now wearing a dark jacket and high crowned hat; I said "How do you do" he replied "How do you do Mr Cox!" he appeared in a frightened and busting way, and said "A fine thing has happened, I have just measured a half bag of potatoes, put them on a donkey at the gate, went in to draw a pint of cider, and on my return the donkey was gone."

I told him that I had just met his son, he asked me where; I said at the bottom of the woods; he asked me twice which one of his son's in an excited manner. I said the short one; and he said Amos.

Young was also holding something in his hand about 12-14 inches long of round appearance, but I did not know what it was, he said something about drenching a pig for Smith, he thanked me and walked on. We came upon the Toll Cottage, where I was told that Hartland was shot, there were several people in the Toll. We arrived home about ten past eight.

Hannah Hartland the wife of Robert Hartland deposed that about seven in the evening I and my husband were sitting in the house, when we heard something at the back by the fowl house, like stones being thrown. I told my husband to go round to see what it was, he lighted a candle, and my little boy followed him. Just as my husband went outside, I saw the flash of a gun on the opposite side of the road, the next moment I saw my poor husband was shot and trying to get back into the house, as soon as he got in he fell down; I moved his clothes and saw the hole in his thigh, and blood running from his wounds. I called for my boys to go and fetch Job Hale and his wife, who live near and cried out "murder" several times. Mrs Hale came and several others soon after. My husband was lifted into bed, the room was a pool of blood.

Mrs Hale- I live about 150 yards from the Toll Gate. I went to Littledean on Saturday evening returning through the Toll gate about seven. I saw Mrs Hartland and spoke to her, when I got about sixty yards from the gate, I heard the report of a gun, which makes a great noise. Shortly after I heard Mrs Hartland scream out.

A servant girl from the George stated that prior to the shooting, William Young the elder had shown her the recognizance papers that he was to be committed for trial for fowl stealing. She had heard him say "I will make him suffer for this before I die, or before I take my trial at Gloucester!
The men who had been detained at Littledean Goal were now on a charge of shooting with intent and removed to Gloucester to stand trial. Amos Young proclaimed his innocence but was found on the 27th March 1852 he was found guilty of murder and sentenced to life, he was removed to Milbank Prison London to await Transportation. William Young Snr was imprisoned and discharged 6th September 1852.

MURDER OF A POLICEMAN 1861

George Cooper 23, Thomas Cooper 29, Richard Roberts 34, Colliers of Coleford and Thomas

Gwilliam 32 Quarryman, were indicted for the wilful murder of Samuel Beard.

It appeared from evidence that Mr Thomas Guest from Littledean, a Farmer, having missed several sheep, and the offence of sheep stealing being rife in the Forest, had given information to Sergeant Beard. Beard undertook to watch Mr Guest's sheep on the 17^h August, who accompanied him around the farm. On the same evening the four prisoners had been drinking together at the Speech House, a well-known inn in the middle of the Forest, and on leaving, Roberts borrowed from the Landlord a large file or rasp, with which he wanted to do some work at home. The four prisoners then left and headed in the direction of Mr Guests land, were they admitted they set nets to catch hares. They were there for some time. Roberts, Gwilliam and George Cooper, were watching at a gate leading into a field where Thomas Cooper was setting the nets. While so occupied, Beard detected Cooper, and seized him, on which he called out to his companions to come to his rescue. The deceased thought Cooper was the sheep stealer of whom he was in search, and endeavoured to take him into custody, but he resisted and a desperate struggle ensured, Cooper using a hedge stake and Beard using his policeman's staff. When the other men came up, however, the odds were too great, and Beard was set upon by the whole party, and received serious and as it turned out, fatal blows to the head and body, the blood flowing profusely from his wounds. At last Beard was overpowered and left senseless on the field. In the meantime Farmer Guest, who did not show much courage concealed himself behind a hedge, and when the fight was over went to look for Beard, but not finding him in the dark and not responding to his shouts left.

The next morning in a corner of the field, Beard lay senseless but still alive and was conveyed home, several cuts were found on his face and head, which it was believed were inflicted by a file. He lingered for a day or two, when death ensured. When on his death bed, he identified all four men.

All four men were apprehended and committed for trial for murder.

The hearing commenced and several witnesses were called. Mr Gunter a Blacksmith living at Carter's Place Berryhill deposed that he was at the Speech House Inn, when the prisoners came in about eight o'clock on the evening of the 17[h] August, and saw Thomas Jarrett an iron refiner of Cinderford give Thomas Gwilliam a file, to which Thomas thanked him.

William Guest repeated the evidence he had given to the coroner, and added, as a reason for not seeing Beard that night as there was a fallen tree between him and where Beard was found lying the next morning. A broken stick lay a few yards away and there were pools of blood in several places. Mr Hatton surgeon who attended Beard described the injuries Beard had received and the following day when a deposition was taken by Mr Brickdale. Supt. Taylor on seeing Beard stated to him that four persons had been apprehended on his deposition and two by two the prisoners were taken to Beard's room who confirmed that they were the men that had beat him. Both Coopers and Gwilliam acquitted Roberts of having any part in the actual attack. Mr Cooke, representing the three men addressed the Jury, begging them to divest themselves of any prejudices with which their minds may have been affected. He argued that Beard, who had evidently gone out for the purpose of detecting sheep stealers, had in a thoughtless and reckless manner interfered with the four men, and brought the unfortunate result upon his own head.

Mr Griffiths the addressed the Jury on behalf of Roberts who stood in the felon's dock on a charge of murder, while there was a strong probability that he took no part in the affray.

After a few minutes consultation the jury found all the prisoners guilty of manslaughter, but recommended Roberts to mercy on the account, of his wife and family. In passing sentence, his Lordship said a most dastardly and cowardly offence had been committed upon an officer of the law, by which he had met his death. Roberts had been recommended to mercy by the jury; but, though he was at all times ready to listen to such recommendations, he could not in this case make any distinction between them. The sentence was that they be kept in penal servitude for the space of fifteen years. Although they were all sent to prison to await transportation it appears that Richard Roberts served out his sentence and was released, while

Thomas Cooper, George Cooper and Thomas Gwilliam were transported on the Clyde to Western Australia, where George Cooper died in 1865 and two years later his brother Thomas in 1867. Thomas Gwilliam died 1914 all in Western Australia.

CENTENARIAN GIPSY'S DEATH 1902

Information has been received of the death of Prudence Smith, a woman of the gipsy tribe, who for some years past, had made Wigpool Green, one of the most out-of-the-way places in the Forest of Dean, her place of abode. The deceased was described as being a widow and her age about 103 years. For two years past she had occupied a cottage with her son Faith Smith, a gipsy. She had been attended by a Doctor at Mitcheldean for bronchitis but she was an inveterate smoker, and to her last breath retained possession of her faculties. The Coroner considered that a post mortem was unnecessary Prudence was buried on the 19th February 1902 at Drybrook, her son Faith Smith died three years later aged 80 and was buried at Walford 15th March 1905.

DEATH FROM A CHERRY STONE 1883

An inquest was held at the Primitive Methodist Chapel Drybrook on the body of Bernard Victor Cowmeadow aged 7 years. The son of Cornelius Cowmeadow, Postmaster Drybrook. It appeared that Bernard went out on a Sunday for a short time and on returning home, he complained of pain in his chest, a few minutes later he died. A post mortem was carried out and a cherry-stone was found in his windpipe and death was caused by suffocation.

KILLED BY TINNED MEAT 1902

An inquest at Cinderford concerning the death of Miriam Buffin aged 30, wife of Sidney Buffin a Collier. From evidence given, Miriam had been confined to bed for around a month, she had been given tinned rabbit, and the following day she had become very ill, a Doctor was called but she died before he could attend her. On opening the inquest Dr Macartney stated, that in his opinion death was due to failure of the heart, the result of intestinal irritation brought on from eating tinned rabbit.

HIGHWAY ROBBERY 1912

A case of highway robbery in which considerable violence, almost amounting to attempted murder happened in the Forest of Dean. Mr E.J.Reece, a Cinderford Grocer had sent his man Henry Andrews aged 50 to deliver goods around the district. Andrews was in charge of a horse and cart loaded with goods to deliver in the Lydbrook district. At about 7 0'clock at night, in rough windy *weather he was making his way back to Cinderford, heading up the steep hill out of Lydbrook towards Mirey Stock, when he was accused by a man named Coles, who asked if he could ride with him back to Cinderford. Andrews recognised the man and allowed him to travel onwards with him. Cole told him that he had urgent business in Cinderford and was bound to get there that night. As they came along by the Swan Inn, Brierley, about half way home, Andrews told Cole that he had to make a call at some cottages to collect some money for his master. Cole very rapidly agreed to take charge, while Andrews collected the money and soon they were on their way again. About ten minutes later they reached Herbert Lodge (Crown workman's residence) when Andrews received a blow to the top of his head and he became blank. Sometime later he came round and found the horse standing quietly some distance nearer to Cinderford, Andrews felt weak and ill but managed to steer the horse and cart. Mr Reece who had been waiting for his return for some time was alarmed and distressed, when he saw the shocking condition Andrews was in. He immediately sent for Dr Mitchell and Inspector Packer. A wound reaching to the bone, nearly 2 inches long, a very jagged ugly cut was duly dressed and Andrews was assisted home to Woodside St, where he gave a statement of events.*

In the early hours of the morning at Lynbrook John Samuel Cole aged 31 lay asleep in his small cottage near the Bell Inn Lynbrook. The Police entered his home and arrested him. Cole protested his innocence, declaring he had been at home all night, he was duly handcuffed and taken to Cinderford. Coles who had married a widow and taken on her five children stood in the Court house a few weeks later, and was found guilty of highway robbery and violence, sentenced to three years penal servitude

Central Lydbrook

Printed in Great Britain
by Amazon